بِسْمِ اللهِ الرَّحْمٰنِ الرَّحِيْمِ

In the name of Allah—The Most Gracious,
The Most Merciful

This journal belongs to

# THE MUSLIM WOMAN'S
## *Journal*

A Book of Reflective Writing Prompts to Inspire a Successful Mindset,
A Life Brimming with Purpose, & a Deeper Connection to Allah

*Kashmir Maryam*

STRANGE
INC

strangeincorporated.org
kashmirmaryam.com

STRANGE
INC

strangeincorporated.org
kashmirmaryam.com

Copyright © 2023 Kashmir Maryam. All rights reserved. No part of this book may be used or reproduced in any manner whatsoever without written permission from the publisher except in the case of a review for a magazine, newspaper, or broadcast. For more information, address Strange Inc Press, New York, NY, 11375.

Published by Strange Inc, a nonprofit publishing house based in New York. Our mission is to elevate the authentic voice of Muslim women.

This book may be purchased for educational, business, or sales promotional use. For information, please e-mail the marketing department at kashmirmaryambookings@gmail.com

*Book cover design by M.Zameer*

ISBN 979-8-9855898-4-9 (Paperback)
ISBN 979-8-9855898-5-6 (Hardcover)
ISBN 979-8-9855898-6-3 (Ebook)

For the sake of The One
who commanded the pen to write

# TABLE *of* CONTENTS

| | |
|---|---|
| *Introduction* | 9 |
| *About This Journal* | 12 |
| 1. For Gratitude | 17 |
| 2. For Finding Your Purpose | 33 |
| 3. For Peace | 55 |
| 4. For Spirituality | 71 |
| 5. For Productivity | 91 |
| 6. For Self-Love | 107 |
| 7. For Romantic Love | 133 |
| 8. For Your Legacy | 157 |
| 9. For the World | 177 |
| 10. For Patience | 189 |
| *The Self-Care Toolkit* | 205 |
| *About the Author* | 209 |

# INTRODUCTION

Peace be upon you, my dear sister. My name is Kashmir, and I am a mother and a wife, as well as a writer and therapist-in-training.

Many cultures view property ownership, marriage, parenting, and white-collar employment as the epitome of "respectability." Even in the present day, these materialistic indicators of "success" persist as a global phenomenon, with many people relentlessly striving their whole lives in pursuit of them. Growing up, I often found myself surrounded by individuals who placed excessive importance on these shallow markers of success. This focus on superficiality left me feeling deeply unsatisfied. *My validation comes from my Creator alone.* I reminded myself of this constantly, even if the people around me didn't understand or appreciate it. I realized that their social norms did not resonate with me because they didn't value the key ingredient of *true* success: God-consciousness. Yes, it's important to be financially stable, but what about the importance of being connected to Allah? Did that no longer have any status? Or did faith take a backseat in the man-made conception of success? Living in the pursuit of these worldly goals alone felt deeply unfulfilling for me. I wanted something *more*. I wanted something to feed my spiritual appetite so that I could wake up in the morning feeling like the richest person alive—and not just because of my bank balance, but because of the fullness of my heart. So that's exactly what I sought out.

My journey toward seeking out the treasure of spiritual connectedness and purpose led me to many different places. But it was adversity and confusion that truly sparked my transformation. It all began at a tumultuous point in my life where I was forced to make a decision that would impact me for the rest of my life. As I concluded my third year of medical school, I found out that I was pregnant with my son. Every inch of my grand life plan had to be reassessed. On one hand, I was contending with the social pressures of following a career that, while respected, did not align with my family values and aspirations. On the other hand, I was struggling to accept that life is full of "unknowns." We plan, but Allah is the best of planners.

*I've worked so hard to get to where I am with my medical education and I'm almost there. The idea of giving that up is scary. Being a doctor is all I've known and I'm not sure I'll find something else that brings me the same level of satisfaction. But, becoming a stay-at-home mom or doing something else instead feels like I'm giving up on my dreams. At the same time, I wonder if this could be the right choice for me to be able to give my future kids the time and attention they need.*

My thoughts were chaotic and confused, but then something shifted. I was on the brink of a big realization. The turning point came when I began to ask myself the all-important questions: what does life mean to me—not to others, but to *me*? For the first time, I delved deeply into my own thoughts and feelings through journaling. It was a transformative experience that would change the course of my life forever. As I wrote more, my focus shifted from activism to self-examination. I began asking myself the most important questions: *who am I, what am I here for, and what comes next?*

In this quest for purpose, I became more self-centered and yet paradoxically more selfless. I started to understand what my soul needed and realized that I wasn't just here to check items off a bucket list, but to *define* the bucket list. I wanted to leave a legacy that was truly my own, and I knew I had only one life to get it right. That's when I realized that the key to all of this was connecting with the Divine. *I needed Allah in my life—now more than ever.*

For years, I had been talking to God through my daily prayers, but it wasn't until I truly started *listening* that things started to change. I watched for His signs and took a leap of faith—*literally*. All I knew at this point was that uncovering my service to the world would be my utmost priority. My job was to seek it out, by any means necessary. And that was exactly what I did. For the first time in my life, I let go of the steering wheel and let God direct me to where *He* wanted me to be, and not where I thought I should be. This is when *Al-Fattah* (The

Opener) opened doors I thought were bolted shut, and closed others that I thought were essential. Through it all I was able to move into what I was *meant* to do all along. But the key to arriving at this place was a journey that stood on the crutches of prayer. As I gazed up at the heavens, I let silent reflection wash over me; my pen danced across the page, filling it with questions. Finally, the answers arrived, and my heart was at peace with them.

Allah was testing me all along. He wanted me to reaffirm my testament of faith "laa ilaaha illAllah", and He wanted to make sure that I was attached to nothing and no one—besides *Him*. He wanted to see me clench onto faith with my molar teeth so that the caliber of my servitude to Him was revealed. This is why I had no option but to write this book. This is my way of paying it forward, so that you can also find the purpose within your own life. What you are holding in your hands is not just a guided journal—it is a blueprint of what your life has been up to this point. But, more importantly, what your life *can* be. It is a guide to discovering *your* unique purpose. And embracing it.

May this journal be the catalyst for your personal growth and success, my dear sister. Let it guide you on your journey toward greatness and transformation. Take this opportunity to embrace your full potential and create the life you've always wanted. The opportunities are limitless and, with Allah's guidance, the power to achieve them lies within *you*.

*Kashmir Maryam — 2023*

# ABOUT this JOURNAL

### Who is This Journal for?

Are you a Muslim woman feeling lost and unsure of your purpose? Are you facing obstacles when it comes to balancing your spiritual and worldly aspirations? This journal is a powerful tool that is designed to guide you on a journey of self-discovery and fulfillment. Unlock answers to questions like "What is my calling?" "What is holding me back from living my dream life?" and "How can I strengthen my connection with Allah while pursuing my aspirations?" Visualize a beautiful future for yourself—in both this world and the next.

Remember, Allah encourages us to constantly seek self-improvement through introspection and contemplation. By setting the intention to journal with the primary goal of deepening your connection with Allah, you can turn the act of writing into a form of worship. Imagine the power of speaking to the Creator of your soul and body, using this journal as a tool for communicating with Him!

### How Can Journaling Help Me?

Journaling is a powerful tool. And it's important to remember that it's not the final destination—it is a *journey*. It will allow you to arrive at a better place spiritually, physically, and even mentally. Therapists often use journaling as a therapeutic tool to help their clients process and make sense of their experiences. By allowing you to bring pen to paper—just as an artist brings brush to canvas—your reflections will become your masterpiece. There are no strict rules or guidelines on *how* or *what* you should write when journaling, making it a beautifully intuitive and intimate experience. Here are some ways that journaling can positively impact you, *insha'Allah*:

- A way to cultivate a deeper relationship with your Creator: Your journal can serve a spiritual place when used to have personal conversations with Allah.
- A tool for healing and self-discovery: Every affliction, fear, or trial we face in our lives serves a deeper purpose. Journaling can help with understanding these experiences and arriving at a more healed place of gratitude and closure.
- A brave way of facing your fears: Your words hold great power, and journaling can be a place of refuge where you are reminded of the strength you have within you.

## How to Use This Journal

This journal is designed to be used in conjunction with *The Muslim Woman's Manifesto: 10 Steps to Achieving Phenomenal Success, in Both Worlds*. It is highly recommended to review the relevant chapters from the manifesto to fully benefit from this journaling experience.

Each chapter of this journal is centered around a specific theme in your life and includes an introduction, an inspiring quote, and a relevant *dua* (prayer) to help focus your thoughts. You'll also find a reference to the corresponding chapter in *The Muslim Woman's Manifesto* for additional context. And last, but certainly not least, you'll also find guided writing prompts for you to journal to; a full page is provided to give you ample space for your responses, allowing you to delve into your thoughts and feelings in as much or as little detail as you'd like to.

Now, brew a tea or coffee and cozy up with this journal. Choose a warm, private spot in your home to write, and pick a time when you can comfortably express your thoughts uninterrupted. Don't worry about the length of what you're writing, just let it come out in whatever way it wants to. When you feel that you've exhausted your thoughts and reflections, close the journal, and return to your regular activities. There are no rules when it comes to the style of your writing—feel free to express yourself through poetry, prose, or even letter form. Be as honest as you can in your responses because authenticity will be essential in properly understanding your unique circumstance. With sincerity and the guidance of Allah, this journaling experience can bring healing, purpose, and a deeper love for your Creator. At the very least, it can help you build momentum toward your goals in life.

Remember, *you* are the author of your journal. The writing prompts are simply a gentle guide for your reflective thinking—but *you* define the narrative. Take your time. Dig deep. And reflect over your responses. Then, use the valuable information in your journal to craft a masterplan for your future, or to make subtle yet impactful changes in your current life. Embrace this opportunity to shape your path forward and enjoy witnessing the transformations that you will experience in your life. Finally, remember that Allah's plan will unfold as it should. So put your full trust in Him and watch the door to boundless opportunities open up for you, *insha'Allah*.

---

*It is important to note that the writing prompts in this journal are not a substitute for the care offered by mental health professionals. If you are experiencing deep and persistent emotional difficulties, please consult your physician or therapist. Some resources for self-care and seeking professional help are provided for you at the end of this book.*

*Sharing your thoughts on this book, in the form of a review, would greatly benefit the author. By sharing your review, you can help ensure that this book continues to find its way into the hands of other readers to benefit from insha'Allah. Scan the QR code to find more information on how you can support the author and this book.*

# 1
## *for*
# GRATITUDE

*When gratitude becomes an essential foundation in our lives, miracles start to appear everywhere.*

—Emmanuel Dagher

Miracles are everywhere. But why is it that some people can see them, yet others cannot? Why is it that some people live in the lap of luxury but feel a deep discomfort gnawing at their soul? And others, in the gutters of poverty, who are the happiest of all? This is because the nourishment of the heart cannot come through materialistic or physical pleasures alone—it can only be satiated by the pursuit of *taqwa* (God-consciousness). And one of the characteristics of someone who possesses *taqwa*, is the act of showing gratitude. Gratitude is what unlocks the heart to see and appreciate the blessings that Allah has showered us with—both within us, and around us. And what we focus on, grows. Rumi said: "The Universe is not outside of you. Look inside yourself; everything that you want, you already are." This is a powerful reminder that much of what we seek externally is already within us—we just have to search for it.

A blessing may not always look the way we expect it to. For example, a reroute from our original intended career could be both a test of our gratitude, as well as a blessing in disguise. While on the external surface it seems like we may have "failed" ourselves by not pursuing a particular career path, it could be that Allah saved us from something that could have been disastrous for our afterlife, as well as for the life of this world. Instead, He granted us something that was better for us—even though it may be difficult to understand this in the moment. The way that we reframe our understanding of our "blessings" is also rooted in trusting Allah, and thus, trusting *His* process—as opposed to our own. This humbles us, as humans have limited vision, both physically and metaphorically. So to be fully grateful—in the truest sense (that Allah is most deserving of), we must treat "gratitude" as more than just a buzzword. We must ponder over it, and self-question where we stand with it. And lastly, we have to be dynamic and malleable in the way that we reframe what has been divinely ordained for us. This multidimensional approach to understanding our blessings and our tests will become the essential foundation of our self-view *and* our worldview. That means that test or trial, can indeed *both* be blessings in disguise—depending on how we frame our understanding of them, and how we choose to respond to them.

This chapter will tap into the different streams and rivers by which blessings are flowing into the ocean of your life. In removing the boulders that block the water pathways, and through purifying the waters themselves, you will become more open to receiving the innumerable blessings as they gush toward you. The goal here is not to accumulate *more*, but to delve deeper into appreciating that which you *already* possess. In doing so, you will realize how full your life *already* is—though society may have you believe otherwise. And naturally, by divine law, Allah will *still* give you more:

> *"If you are thankful, I will give you more."*
> (The Qur'an, 14:7)

The reflective questions that you will soon be answering will help you to recenter your perspective around everything you currently possess, both in your hands as well as *within* yourself. Without any further ado, let us begin.

**Read:** *"Count Your Blessings"* from *The Muslim Woman's Manifesto*

**Dua:**

رَبِّ أَوْزِعْنِىٓ أَنْ أَشْكُرَ نِعْمَتَكَ ٱلَّتِىٓ أَنْعَمْتَ عَلَىَّ وَعَلَىٰ وَٰلِدَىَّ وَأَنْ أَعْمَلَ صَٰلِحًا تَرْضَىٰهُ وَأَدْخِلْنِى بِرَحْمَتِكَ فِى عِبَادِكَ ٱلصَّٰلِحِينَ

**Pronunciation:** *Rabbi awzi'ni an-ashkura ni'matakallati an'amta alayya wa ala waaliadyya wa an a'mala saalihann tardaahu wa'adkhilni bi rahmatika fee ibaadika-saliheen*

**Meaning:** My Lord! Inspire me to always be thankful for Your favors that You have bestowed upon me and upon my parents, and to do good deeds that please You. Admit me, by Your mercy, into the company of Your righteous servants.

**Reference:** The Qur'an, 27:19

*Journaling*
PROMPTS

# What are 20 things (or more) that you are grateful to Allah for giving you?

*What steps do you currently take to foster and deepen a feeling of gratitude in your connection with Allah?*

What are 20 things (or more) that you are grateful to Allah for not giving you?

*Reflect over the things that Allah did not ordain for you to have. Perhaps at the time, you did not understand the wisdom behind it, but in hindsight you see things differently.*

# What is your biggest achievement?

*What feelings does this achievement evoke in you? What makes this a "big" achievement for you? In what ways could this achievement be of benefit to you in the akhirah (the life of the hereafter)?*

# What is the most meaningful thing that anyone has ever done for you?

*What made this experience meaningful for you? What do you think made this individual do something like this for you? How did it make you feel?*

Can you think of three instances in your past where you underestimated or overlooked something or someone?

*What factors do you believe contributed to your tendency to take these moments for granted? How can you practice more gratitude in similar situations in the future?*

# What are three things that Allah saved you from?

*We often consider blessings to be positive events or outcomes, but sometimes Allah's protection can also be a blessing in disguise. Can you think of three instances where Allah saved you from something that could have had negative consequences for you?*

# What are five unique qualities or features that make your home feel like a special place?

*What does "home" feel like to you? What are the sensory details (such as sight, sound, and smell) that contribute to the feeling of home for you? How can you enhance the special and personal qualities of your home?*

Can you think of three individuals in your life who have had a significant positive impact on you, and for whom you are particularly grateful?

*What are the specific qualities or actions of these individuals that make them important and meaningful to you, and for which you are grateful? How can you express your gratitude toward them for their presence in your life? Can you think of some individuals who value your presence in their lives and for whom you are thankful?*

# What are 10 thoughts that motivate you to start your day?

*Can you give an example of a powerful thought that sets the tone for a successful day?*

Can you think of 10 specific thoughts or affirmations that may help you to relax and let go of any stress or worries, and allow you to sleep more easily and peacefully at night?

*Going to sleep with good thoughts can help to reduce stress and anxiety, relax the mind and body, improve the quality of sleep, and set a positive tone for the next day.*

Can you identify five specific qualities or characteristics that distinguish you from others and make you unique?

*Why do these qualities or characteristics hold value or meaning for you, and how do they contribute to your sense of self and personal identity?*

Can you think of 20 specific things that bring you joy and make you feel happy?

*What are the characteristics or qualities of these things that contribute to your happiness? Are they people, places, possessions, or memories? How do you define and experience "happiness," and how do these things fit into your definition and experience of happiness?*

# 2
## *for*
# FINDING YOUR PURPOSE

*There is no greater gift you can give or receive than to honor your calling. It's why you were born. And how you become most truly alive.*

—Oprah Winfrey

Purpose is something that most people will spend their lifetime seeking. So be patient with yourself and remember that there is no timeline on "purpose" as long as you think deeply about it on a daily basis. But imagine *if* there was a way that you could expedite the time you spent in its pursuit? What *if* there was a divinely mapped guideline of what the foundation of your purpose should be based on? Imagine how much more fulfillment you would find in your life, if only you surrendered to it. But first, in envisioning what could *be*, we must first loosen our attachment to what *was*.

Purpose, coupled with sincerity, is something so integral to the life of a Muslim. By its nature, it is infused into all that we do. We seek it out in every prayer that we make: "Guide us along the straight path." (*The Qur'an 1:6*). This means that we ask only of Allah—whose knowledge encompasses all things—to guide us in our pursuit of purpose in both worldly and spiritual matters. And if we have anchored our intention in sincerity, we *must* trust that Allah will guide us.

Our purpose provides an enlightened map to guide us through the confusing and murky waters of unclarity. It provides a reason. A *meaning*. For each of us, this journey is unique, and will undoubtedly involve unexpected twists and turns. Therefore, this chapter's journaling prompts focus on what purpose looks like for *you*. The questions are specific but will also focus on the elements of your life that can help to bring purpose to the forefront in a way that you may not have considered before. For this reason, there are more prompts in this chapter than anywhere else in this book. This is because our purpose is imperative in understanding our very existence.

Self-discovery is a winding path that may present us with detours, reversals, and unexpected turns—we will encounter obstacles and setbacks that test our resilience and faith. Use these challenges as opportunities for growth and introspection. In these moments, you should trust your senses and intuition, and *always* seek guidance from Allah. So, embrace the journal prompts in this chapter as a chance to uncover your personal purpose and how it shapes your journey in self-development.

**Read:** "Find Your Purpose" from *The Muslim Woman's Manifesto*

**Dua:**

رَبِّ أَعِنِّي وَلاَ تُعِنْ عَلَىَّ وَانْصُرْنِي وَلاَ تَنْصُرْ عَلَىَّ وَامْكُرْ لِي وَلاَ تَمْكُرْ عَلَىَّ وَاهْدِنِي وَيَسِّرْ هُدَايَ إِلَيَّ وَانْصُرْنِي عَلَى مَنْ بَغَى عَلَىَّ اللَّهُمَّ اجْعَلْنِي لَكَ شَاكِرًا لَكَ ذَاكِرًا لَكَ رَاهِبًا لَكَ مِطْوَاعًا إِلَيْكَ مُخْبِتًا أَوْ مُنِيبًا رَبِّ تَقَبَّلْ تَوْبَتِي وَاغْسِلْ حَوْبَتِي وَأَجِبْ دَعْوَتِي وَثَبِّتْ حُجَّتِي وَاهْدِ قَلْبِي وَسَدِّدْ لِسَانِي وَاسْلُلْ سَخِيمَةَ قَلْبِي

**Pronunciation:** *Rabbi a'innii wa laa tu'in 'alayy(a), wan-surnii wa laa tansur 'alayy(a), wam-kur lii wa laa tamkur 'alayy(a), wah-dinii wa yassir hudaya ilayya, wan-surnii 'alaa man baghaa 'alayy(a). Allahummaj-'alnii laka shaakiran, laka dhakiran, laka raahibann, laka mitwaa'a, ilayka mukhbitan, aw-muniibann. Rabba taqabbal tawbatii, wagh-sil hawbatii, wa ajib da'watii, wa thabbit hujjatii, wah-di qalbii, wa saddid lisaani, was-lul sakheemata qalbi*

**Meaning:** My Lord, help me and do not give help against me. Grant me victory, and do not grant victory over me. Plan on my behalf and do not plan against me. Guide me and make right guidance easy for me. Grant me victory over those who act wrongfully towards me. Oh Allah, make me grateful to You, mindful of You, full of fear towards You, devoted to Your obedience, humble before You. My Lord, accept my repentance, wash away my sins, answer my supplication, clearly establish my evidence, guide my heart, make true my tongue and draw out malice in my breast.

**Reference:** Sunan Abi Dawud 1510

*Journaling* PROMPTS

# If you were to wake up tomorrow morning, and live your "dream life," what would it look like?

*Imagine being able to live your "dream life" without any financial or responsibility limitations. What would your career be in this dream life? How would your spiritual life look? What decisions would you make that you might not be able to make now?*

# What are 20 goals or aspirations you want to achieve before the end of your life?

*What is the significance of each item on this list for you, and what are some small steps you can take to make progress toward achieving them?*

# What do you see as the meaning or purpose of your life?

*Reflect on what drives you, what you value, and what you hope to achieve in this lifetime.*

What are some activities or projects that you are passionate about and enjoy spending your time on? Do these align with your strengths or areas of expertise?

*Do you have any ideas for how you could utilize your skills and talents in a side project or personal venture?*

# In what ways do you believe your skills and talents could be utilized in a professional setting?

*Are there any specific career paths or roles that you think would be a good fit for your abilities?*

Which aspects of your life do you feel are most in need of development or growth, and why do you feel that way?

*You might consider areas such as spirituality, romantic love, career and work-life balance, mental and physical health, and family life.*

What are your top five spiritual goals for this coming year? And what are your top five worldly goals?

*Next to each goal, describe:*
*1. Why is this goal important to me?*
*2. What steps can I take toward achieving this goal?*

If you had the opportunity to make two wishes, one for your present life and one for the afterlife, what would they be?

*Please take the time to carefully reflect on your wishes. If you have more than one, you are welcome to include all of them. You may choose to utilize these wishes in your dua.*

# What values or priorities guide your decisions and actions in life?

*Consider the values or priorities that shape your choices and actions in life. Are there any discrepancies between your values and actions? Make adjustments accordingly.*

# Why do you *choose* to be a Muslim?

*Could you elaborate on the aspects of Islam that resonate most with you and align with your personal values and beliefs? What about this faith speaks to you on a deeper level?*

What are 10 things that give you hope, inspiration, or a sense of excitement about the future?

*These could be personal, professional, or societal goals or aspirations that you are looking forward to.*

# What are five things that cause you fear or anxiety about the future?

*For each of these things, could you describe what specifically scares you about it and what steps you could take to feel more secure or reassured about it?*

# What gives you a sense of purpose or direction in life?

*What inspires or motivates you to take action and make progress toward your goals?*

Is there a particular subject or area of study that you feel would enrich your life or help you to achieve your goals?

*Could you commit to setting aside some time in the coming week to explore this topic further and see how it resonates with you?*

# What do you believe is your unique contribution or value that you bring to the world?

*What evidence or experiences support this belief? Are there multiple areas where you feel you could make a positive impact, or is there a particular service or offering that you are particularly passionate about? Please remember that your contribution to the world can include something like taking care of your family and home—this is also a revolutionary act.*

# What are some things you learned about your *spiritual self*?

*Describe the kind of relationship you have with your soul.*

# What are some things you have learned about your *physical self*?

*Describe the kind of relationship you have with your physical body.*

# What are some things you have learned about your mental health?

*Describe the kind of relationship you have with your mind.*

# 3

*for*
# PEACE

*Verily, in the remembrance of Allah do hearts find rest.*
(The Qur'an, 13:28)

*Peace of mind* is a treasure. When the heart has found refuge in the caves of peace, it is deeply content. It is still. It is calm and unperturbed by worldly wants. Instead, it is full of richness—without necessarily needing to possess anything materialistically. It is Divinely placed through the remembrance of Allah. And it is indeed one of the most underrated aspects of living a *phenomenal* existence.

You see, it is so easy to become overwhelmed and distracted by the perpetual noise we are surrounded by. We often get so used to the babel of sound in the busy day-to-day hustle that we have normalized the pinging notifications, and electronic humming of engines and appliances in our modern world. We rarely stop to "smell the roses." This is why *peace* is such a sought-after commodity. It is so precious that even the materially wealthy among us quickly realize that living luxuriously becomes hollow and empty when it is not tempered by something deeper. What most do not realize, is that the currency by which peace is brought is through spirituality—not through bitcoin, or the dollar.

Perhaps one of the most poignant moments in appreciating peace, for me personally, was throughout the recent global pandemic. A few months into lockdown, birdsongs could be heard more clearly in neighborhoods where their chirping had been drowned out for many years. Living in a busy city neighborhood in Philadelphia, I was so unaccustomed to hearing the beautiful sounds of nature. The inescapable commotion of technology and automobiles being replaced with the harmonious melody of little birds made me realize how much clamor (metaphorical and otherwise) I had in my own life. So, this chapter asks questions that will help you consider what "noise" you may have in your life—and on the contrary, identifying where "peace" can be found. This peace expands beyond our external sensory world and flows into our internal spiritual world. In order to achieve *true* success, the two must have a collaborative relationship, and be given unique and special attention.

Attaining a harmonious relationship between our spiritual and physical existence leads to a harmonious state of mind, body, and spirit. The following writing prompts will encourage you to consider the things you must let go of. This may include possessions, people, and even circumstances that may be chipping away at your inner peace. As with all clutter, there must be a place—a compartment into which that thing must be organized and placed. In my own personal life, I have found that writing out these thoughts has given me great clarity—it has allowed my inner thoughts to find a voice through pen and paper. Once these thoughts were written out in detail, I found that organizing them became much easier—in fact, there was something therapeutic and healing in this process. During a particularly chaotic period in my life, I confided in my brother about how I was feeling; he responded with some simple and monumental words—he asked me, "Have you written everything out? If you write out everything on your mind, you will feel better." Without exaggeration, his advice changed my life. For this reason, I propose the same to you.

**Read:** "Clean House" from *The Muslim Woman's Manifesto*

**Dua:**

اللَّهُمَّ أَنْتَ السَّلَامُ وَمِنْكَ السَّلَامُ تَبَارَكْتَ ذَا الْجَلَالِ وَالْإِكْرَامِ

**Pronunciation:** *Allahumma Antassalaam wa minkassalaam, tabaarakta thul jalaali, wal ikraam*

**Meaning:** Oh Allah, You are Peace and from You is peace. Blessed are You, The Majestic and Noble.

**Reference:** Sahih Muslim 592

*Journaling*
PROMPTS

# Is there an area of your life that feels disorganized or cluttered?

*Consider spiritual as well as material aspects. Set aside dedicated time for each area of your life that you want to address or prioritize.*

# What are some things or people that you need to release in order to move forward?

*What negative influences are hindering your spiritual growth? What are you clinging to that you know is detrimental to your well-being? What reasons do you have for letting go of these things or people?*

# What are 20 of the most meaningful or important lessons you have learned in your life up to this point?

*Think about the experiences and events that have taught you valuable insights, and the knowledge and wisdom that you have gained. Think about the lessons that have been the most difficult to learn, the ones that have come from failure, or the ones that have been the most important in shaping your worldview.*

# What are some personal habits or behaviors that you would like to modify or improve?

*Describe the habits that are most important to you. Why are they important to you? What small steps can you take to start working on these habits?*

# Write a letter to your younger self.

*What are some things you wish your younger self would have known? What are some things you wish you had known or done differently when you were younger?*

# What is an incredibly difficult decision you have had to make in your life?

*What was difficult about this decision? Do you feel that you made the right choice? Why, or why not? What are some strategies or actions you can take to cope with and heal from potential emotional wounds caused by this decision.*

# How do you approach your prayers in terms of concentration and mindfulness (*Khushoo'*)?

*What strategies or resources can you use to improve your focus during prayer? Do you have a good understanding of the Arabic words you are reciting during prayer? Do you have access to an easy-to-read translation of the Qur'an?*

Write a letter to someone from your past who has caused you harm or pain.

*In the letter, describe the ways in which this person hurt you and what you would like to say to them now. You can choose to send the letter or keep it for yourself. The objective of this exercise is to find resolution and healing from past hurts.*

# What is a challenge you have recently overcome that you need to give yourself credit for?

*What helped you to overcome this challenge?*

# Is there something from your past that makes you feel sad or unhappy?

*You can be as vulnerable as you would like with this. If so, what are they and how do they make you feel? Do you have any ways of managing these feelings of sadness when they come up?*

# What brings you a sense of calm and serenity?

*Why do these things have this effect on you?*

# 4
## *for*
# SPIRITUALITY

*We are not human beings having a spiritual experience. We are spiritual beings having a human experience.*

—Pierre Teilhard de Chardin

Hasan Al-Basri, a renowned scholar from the early generation of Muslims (the *tabi'un*), once said: "As much as you fix your *salah* (the five daily prayers), your life will be fixed. Did you not know that *salah* was equated with Success: 'Come to Prayer, Come to Success.'"

The correlation between what your life looks like right now and the presence or absence of your prayers is deeply interconnected; this theme in your life defines *everything*. Submission to God, through prayer, is only *one* of the ways by which we can become closer to Him—and this chapter will offer you a clarifying insight into where you may currently stand in that relationship.

It can be difficult to be vulnerable on paper with this subject. We may not be ready to face our inner demons. At times we may even be living an existence where we are afraid to tap into the spiritual aspect of our life so we distract ourselves with other active pursuits—with work, studies, overconsumption of food and social media, just to name a few. But deep down something will always be gnawing at our soul if we do not address this aspect of our existence. *This is your soul speaking to you*. This feeling of being unfulfilled in the deepest sense is your soul telling you that it needs something *more*. It years for a healthy relationship with the heart and with The One who created that very heart. It craves something greater than anything that the worldly life can offer. *Do not ignore this voice.* It will only get louder and louder until it is given what it desires. This chapter invites you to explore the longing of your soul. Remember, Allah eagerly awaits a profound connection with you, but the journey towards it starts with a single step taken by *you*.

**Read:** "Find Power in Prayer" from *The Muslim Woman's Manifesto*

**Dua:**

يَا مُقَلِّبَ الْقُلُوبِ ثَبِّتْ قَلْبِى عَلَى دِينِكَ

**Pronunciation:** *Yaa Muqallib al-Quloob, thabbit qalbee 'alaa deenik*

**Translation:** Oh Turner of the Hearts (Allah, the Most High), keep our hearts firm upon your religion

**Reference:** Sahih Muslim 6418

*Journaling*
PROMPTS

Describe a time in your life when you felt most connected to Allah.

*What did this feel like? What do you think made you feel so connected to Allah in this moment? What actions can you take to cultivate a deeper sense of spirituality?*

If you had the opportunity to meet the Prophet Muhammad (peace be upon him), what message or words of appreciation would you want to convey to him?

*Reflect on the impact of his teachings and actions on your life and the world. Think about the lessons and wisdom that you have learned from him and the way he lived his life. This is also an opportunity to express admiration for his character, leadership, and his role as a Messenger of Allah (peace be upon him).*

# Which female figure from Islamic history do you find most inspiring?

*What specific characteristics or qualities of this woman do you admire the most, and how can you strive to embody them in your own life?*

# Can you recall a recent experience that moved you to tears?

*What was the situation and what emotions did it evoke in you? How did you feel once the tears had passed?*

How many of Allah's 99 names are you familiar with? List as many as you can and provide the meanings of each.

*Making an effort to learn and use Allah's unique names in your dua can have a transformative effect on your life. Why not take the time to learn all of Allah's names and enrich your spiritual practice by incorporating them into your daily supplications?*

# What are your favorite chapters or verses from the Qur'an, and why do they hold a special place in your heart?

*Are there any verses that particularly resonate with you at this stage in your life or that inspire a deep sense of love and devotion for Allah? Which verses give you hope in Allah's mercy?*

# Finish the following sentence: "Oh Allah, forgive me for..."

*This is an important step in the process of self-improvement and spiritual growth. Additionally, it is an act of humility and submission to Allah, recognizing that we are not perfect and that we depend on His forgiveness.*

# How would you describe your current relationship with Allah?

*Are there any areas in which you feel you could improve this relationship? What steps can you take to strengthen your connection with Allah and bring you closer to Him? Conversely, are there any behaviors or actions that may be hindering your spiritual growth and sense of closeness to Allah? Consider devoting time over the coming days to identify and work on these actionable steps toward deepening your bond with Him.*

# When you pray, what do you *feel*?

*Are there any emotions that are present or absent during this time? How do you feel after completing your prayers? If you happen to miss a prayer, how do you typically feel and what do you believe may be contributing factors to this emotional response?*

# What distractions prevent you from fully focusing on and connecting with Allah?

*How can you effectively eliminate or minimize these distractions and cultivate a greater sense of spiritual presence and connection?*

Who are the people in your life who help you feel closer to Allah, and what is it about them that promotes this sense of spiritual connection?

*How can you strive to embody similar qualities and behaviors in your own life to foster a deeper connection with Allah?*

# What does the concept of "spirituality" mean to you?

*How does your "spirituality" show up in everyday life?*

What are you currently feeling afraid of, and how can relying on Allah and seeking His guidance and support help you to overcome this fear?

*Identify and acknowledge the source of your fear and to understand how it is affecting your thoughts, feelings, and actions. Reflect on the role of faith and spiritual practices in addressing and coping with your fears. Allah is the ultimate protector and guide and seeking His help will give you peace of mind.*

Do you feel like there are aspects of your Islamic practice that have become routine or mechanical, rather than truly meaningful and heartfelt?

*What could you do to rejuvenate and deepen your spiritual bond with Allah in these areas?*

Can you recall a specific instance in your life when prayer had a powerful and transformative impact on you?

*How did this experience illustrate the strength and efficacy of prayer in your life?*

# Where do you feel most connected to Allah?

*What is it about this place (or places) that enhances your spiritual awareness and sense of closeness to Him?*

Upon your passing, what is one thing that you hope people will remember and say about you? This doesn't have to be true at present, but rather a goal or aspiration that you can work toward, *inshaAllah*.

*As the day of your funeral will inevitably arrive, consider how you can prepare for it and make sure that your legacy reflects the values and ideals that are most important to you.*

# 5
## *for*
# PRODUCTIVITY

*The bad news is time flies.*
*The good news is you're the pilot.*
—Michael Altshuler

*Time* is a finite commodity. And just like any other resource that is limited in supply, it is extremely precious in value. However, *time* itself is not the determinant of success. Rather, it is *how* it is used—or spent. Fortunately, as Muslims we have an absolute edge on this. The Qur'an and the *sunnah* (the traditions of the Prophet Muhammad (peace be upon him)) offer clear guidance on how to structure our time in the most productive and meaningful way. To effectively manage our time and maximize productivity, we need only look to the guidance and examples set by Allah through these sources.

This chapter will allow you to explore how you are presently utilizing your time. You will also be encouraged to consider your habits around productivity, as well as how you are "budgeting" your time—just as you would any other type of currency.

Routine and structure in your day are the backbone for productive habits to flourish. However, it is important to remember to pause and reflect on the purpose of it all. It is not enough to want to complete endless checklists from dawn till dusk. Rather, it is more efficient to use specific pockets of the day for the tasks that are most optimal for *your* desired lifestyle—there is no "one-size-fits-all."

After responding to the prompts in this chapter, I encourage you to reflect over your answers. Once you have pondered over your thoughts on this topic, you will have the opportunity to assess the areas about productivity that you would like to devote more time to working on. I encourage you to also use your responses as an instruction manual for curating the lifestyle you aspire toward—one that involves an acknowledgement of your strengths as well as your challenges.

**Read:** "Take Control of Your Time" from *The Muslim Woman's Manifesto*

**Dua:**

أَصْبَحْنَا وَأَصْبَحَ الْمُلْكُ لِلَّهِ رَبِّ الْعَالَمِينَ اللَّهُمَّ إِنِّي أَسْأَلُكَ خَيْرَ هَذَا الْيَوْمِ فَتْحَهُ وَنَصْرَهُ وَنُورَهُ وَبَرَكَتَهُ وَهُدَاهُ وَأَعُوذُ بِكَ مِنْ شَرِّ مَا فِيهِ وَشَرِّ مَا بَعْدَهُ

**Pronunciation:** *Asbah'na, wa asbahal mulku lillahi rabbil aalameen. Allahumma inni as'aluka khayra haathal-yawm fat'ha, wa nasrahu, wa nooruhu, wa barakatuh, wa hudaa'hu, wa a'oothu bika min sharri maa feehi, wa sharri maa ba'dah*

**Meaning:** We have reached the morning, and in the morning the dominion belongs to Allah, the Lord of the universe. Oh Allah! I ask You for the good this day contains, for conquest, victory, light, blessing and guidance during it; and I seek refuge in You from the evil it contains, and the evil contained in what comes after it.

**Reference:** Sunan Abi Dawud 5084

*Journaling*
PROMPTS

Is there something that you have been putting off or procrastinating on, despite knowing that it needs to be done?

*What thoughts or beliefs hold you back from taking immediate action? How does procrastination make you feel? On the other hand, what mental shift or mindset helps you to overcome inaction and motivates you to complete the task? How do you feel after finishing it?*

# What are the top five priorities in your life at present, and why are they most important to you?

*Are you actively making time and space in your life for these priorities? If not, what small steps can you take to begin incorporating these priorities into your daily routine and making them a more integral part of your life?*

# Are there any particular acts of worship that you wish you had more time for?

*Why are these practices important to you, and how might you be able to find space for them within your current schedule and daily routine?*

# What does your current morning routine involve, and how might you like to improve or enhance it?

*Could waking up earlier to perform the tahajjud (night prayer) be a possibility? If so, what steps or changes to your current routine would need to be made to make this more feasible and achievable?*

# What activities or tasks tend to occupy the majority of your time?

*How much of your time is spent consuming content versus actively engaging in productivity or creative endeavors? How much time do you dedicate to ibaadah (worship) and spiritual growth? What areas of your life are most impacted by the allocation of your time in this way?*

What distractions or time-consuming habits currently present in your life do not contribute to your overall well-being and sense of balance?

*How can you take active steps to eliminate or minimize these distractions and free up time for activities that are more nourishing and enriching?*

# How do you currently spend your leisure or "free" time?

*How would you like to utilize this time in the future?*

# How do you feel about your relationship with technology and social media?

*Approximately how many hours a day do you spend using your phone and engaging with social media? You may find it helpful to use the activity tracker on your phone to get a more detailed breakdown of your phone usage habits.*

## How do you typically organize the tasks and responsibilities you need to complete?

*Do you prioritize your to-do list or use a standard checklist? Consider trying out the technique of time-blocking, which involves setting aside specific blocks of time to focus on specific tasks, as a way to help you effectively manage your responsibilities and work through your task list.*

What are the habits, behaviors, actions, or deeds that you would like to stop doing and why?

*How can you actively work to eliminate these from your life?*

Are there any tasks or responsibilities that you could potentially delegate or outsource to others in order to lighten your workload and allow you to focus on your most important priorities?

*It can be helpful to remember that it is okay to ask for help and that seeking assistance from others is a perfectly valid and effective way to manage your time and responsibilities.*

## What does "balance" mean to you personally? How do you define a balanced lifestyle?

*Can you envision what a typical day or schedule would look like for you if you were able to achieve a sense of balance in your life?*

What are three ways in which you can actively practice surrendering to Allah in your life?

*Do you struggle with relinquishing control and letting go? If so, what makes this difficult for you? What specific things are you currently trying to control in your life that you could instead entrust to Allah's care and guidance?*

# 6
## *for*
## SELF-LOVE

*If I am not good to myself, how can I expect anyone else to be good to me?*

—Maya Angelou

Loving oneself is often conflated with beauty rituals and the external embellishments of self-care. However, self-love is much deeper than that. It involves our inner voice. How we speak to ourselves. How we take care of our mental health, as well as our spiritual and physical body. It is about how we make space and show up for ourselves. Self-care is also about how we heal from the painful events in our past. But most importantly, self-love should be what we feel when we look deep into the mirror—at both our body, and our soul.

I want you to enjoy writing this chapter. I want you to pamper yourself with patience and the promise to do the best for your body *and* your soul. I want you to remember that self-love is a life-long pursuit, and there will be moments in your existence where you *will* fall short in this. You *will* feel deflated at times. Unworthy. Half empty. But what will carry you through this vulnerability is enduring in your commitment to give rights to the different dimensions of you: to your flesh, your bones, your spirit, and your mental health. Looking after these facets of yourself can only happen when you make a steadfast commitment to self-love—in the deepest sense of the word. And you *must* make it a lifelong pursuit. No one else can do this job for you. Once you have this relationship with yourself, you will be more forgiving of your shortcomings, and more hopeful in Allah's compassion. You will show more grace towards your imperfections, and you'll be gentler with your healing.

**Read:** "Make Yourself a Priority" from *The Muslim Woman's Manifesto*

**Dua:**

اللهم أنت حسنت خلقي فحسن خُلُقي

**Pronunciation:** *Allahumma Anta hassanta khalqi fa hassin khuluqi*

**Meaning:** Oh Allah, You have beautified my body, so beautify my character.

**Reference:** Saḥiḥ Ibn Ḥibban 6734

*Journaling*
PROMPTS

Compose a list of 20 positive affirmations that encourage and inspire you.

*These can be statements that reflect your goals, values, or desired qualities. Examples may include "I am worthy and deserving," "I am strong and capable," "I am loved and valued," or "I am confident in my abilities." These affirmations can serve as a source of motivation and encouragement as you work toward your desired future self.*

What are you most afraid of about yourself, and why does this fear concern you?

*What helps alleviate or overcome this fear? How are you dealing with this fear currently, and what could help you overcome it?*

What are some things about yourself that you love or appreciate the most, and why do you love these things about yourself?

*What makes something "worthy" or "deserving" of love in your opinion? What characteristics do you most admire and appreciate in others?*

# Compose a love letter to your body, expressing appreciation and love for all that it does for you.

*This can take the form of a poem, prose, or any other creative style that feels authentic and meaningful to you. This letter can be a way to celebrate and honor the unique qualities and abilities of your body and to express gratitude for all that it does for you.*

Compose a love letter to your soul, expressing appreciation and love for all that it is and all that it brings to your life.

*This can take the form of a poem, prose, or any other creative style that feels authentic and meaningful to you.*

# What is something that you need to forgive yourself for?

*Have you been carrying this burden for a long time? Why have you not been able to forgive yourself for this yet? What could help you to let go of this guilt or self-blame and move forward with self-forgiveness?*

When you are experiencing pain or hardship, what are some kind and compassionate ways that you can take care of yourself?

*Are you treating yourself with kindness and compassion during tough times, or are there ways to offer yourself more gentleness and understanding?*

# How can you tell when your spiritual self is being neglected?

*What can you do for yourself in these moments?*

# How do you remind yourself that you are *enough*?

*Has anyone ever made you feel inadequate? How did it impact you? What daily affirmations or actions can you take to remind yourself of your worth and that you are enough?*

Describe a "failure" that you experienced. Why do you feel that this was a "failure"?

*In hindsight, what have you learned or gained from this experience? How has it shaped or influenced your growth or perspective?*

What are the potential benefits and impacts of prioritizing yourself and your own well-being?

*How might this shift in focus also positively affect the lives of others around you?*

What are three habits or practices that are no longer serving you or bringing value to your life?

*How can you release or let go of these?*

# What helps you to slow down and feel more present?

*Can you give an example of an activity that helps you feel most present? How does being present impact your overall well-being?*

How do you typically go about seeking support or help when you need it, and do you often struggle with asking for assistance?

*If so, what might be some of the underlying reasons or barriers that make it difficult for you to ask for support?*

# How do you notice "burn-out" when you are getting close to it?

*When you have burned out, how does that feel? Describe the impact(s) that it has on your body, your mental health, and your spiritual self.*

# What are some ways that you can celebrate and honor yourself today?

*How can you incorporate self-care activities into your daily routine?*

Write a list of all the things that you would like to say "no" to in your life. How many of these are you currently able to say "no" to, and why or why not?

*What might be some of the obstacles or challenges that make it difficult for you to assert boundaries or say "no" in certain situations?*

Create a list of all the things that you would like to say "yes" to in your life.

*How many of these are you currently doing? What might be some of the factors or considerations that influence your decisions to say "yes" to certain opportunities or experiences?*

# What are some current sources of stress in your life, both short-term and long-term?

*Why do these things cause you stress, and what are some potential ways to address or manage these stressors?*

# What three practices you can implement in your life to reduce stress?

*How do you manage yourself in moments of high stress? In what ways could you improve on your response to stress? Focus on implementing these practices into your day.*

# What have you done lately that you are proud of?

*What makes you proud of this? Do you celebrate your own successes?*

# What are your goals for the year ahead?

*Make a list of at least ten things that you would like to achieve in the coming year. Be specific and realistic in your goal setting. Use this exercise to understand your priorities and the things that are most meaningful to you.*

# What does your perfect self-care day look like?

*Consider ways that you can nurture the different parts of your Self—including your spiritual, your physical, and your intellectual self.*

# 7
## *for*
# ROMANTIC LOVE

*Love cures people—both the ones who
give it and the ones who receive it.*

—Karl A. Menninger

Love colors the world in a way that no other emotion can. When we have loving and nurturing people around us to share our special moments with, it turns our perspective of life into something hopeful. Who we choose to spend these moments with heavily defines the trajectory of our life, since we are a careful summation of the company we keep. In this chapter, we will explore the importance of fostering strong, loving relationships with our spouses, and the value of cultivating deep connections with our loved ones.

The Prophet Muhammad (peace be upon him) exemplified love and compassion in all of his relationships—both domestically with his family, and publicly, with his companions. Despite facing challenges and conflicts with loved ones, he always turned to Allah for guidance and showed love and understanding toward them, peace be upon him. A significant lesson to be gleaned from this is that no one is immune to tests and trials in their relationships. However, by acknowledging our own frailties and how they may affect our connections, we can embark on a path towards forgiveness and empathy. Cultivating better relationships requires perseverance and fortitude in a transient world, but the guidance from our Creator serves as a beacon of light; the

Qur'an reminds us of our imperfections and inspires us to strive for growth and improvement in *all* of our interpersonal dealings.

In the previous chapter, we delved into the realm of self-love. Now, it's time to assess the state of our relationships and discover ways to enhance and elevate them. By deepening our self-awareness and understanding our unique love language, it will pave the way for us to enhance our relationships and create deeper connections with those around us. These improved relationships bring with them a multitude of benefits that enrich our lives in numerous ways. Firstly, they become more fulfilling as we can connect on a deeper level, understand each other's needs and emotions better, and resolve conflicts in a more harmonious manner. Secondly, our relationships become more satisfying as we experience greater closeness and intimacy with our loved ones. Thirdly, they become more meaningful as we can build strong bonds based on mutual trust, respect, and love. These enriched relationships enable us to lead a more joyful life as we are surrounded by people who bring us happiness, comfort, and support; by focusing on our relationships and working to make them the best they can be, we can elevate our overall well-being and live a life filled with happiness and fulfillment.

**Read:** "Revolutionize Your Marriage" from *The Muslim Woman's Manifesto*

**Dua:**

رَبِّ إِنِّى لِمَآ أَنزَلْتَ إِلَىَّ مِنْ خَيْرٍ فَقِيرٌ

**Pronunciation:** *Rabbi inni lima anzalta ilayya min khairin faqeer*

**Meaning:** My Lord! Truly, I am in need of whatever good that You bestow on me.

**Reference:** The Qur'an, 28:24

*Journaling*
PROMPTS

# What are your feelings about your current relationship status?

*Are you blissfully single, divorced, widowed, separated, married or seeking marriage? How does your relationship status shape your life? What is your "dream" relationship status?*

# What does a thriving, nourishing marriage look like to you?

*If you are not married, please apply this prompt to a platonic relationship (with a loved one). What attributes do you believe contribute to a healthy relationship? How does being in a healthy relationship make you feel? In what ways can it enrich your life?*

# What are the characteristics of a toxic / destructive marriage to you?

*If you are not married, please apply this prompt to a platonic relationship (with a loved one). How does being in a toxic relationship make you feel? In what ways can it damage your life? Are you currently in a toxic relationship? What are some warning signs that a relationship might be unhealthy?*

# Write a poem for your husband, and present it to him as a heartfelt gift.

*If you are not married, craft a poem for a loved one and surprise them with your words of love and appreciation.*

# What is "love" to you?

*What are the traits that define a loving person? How do they express their love through their words and actions? What kind of gestures or behaviors demonstrate love? How do you experience love in your own life?*

# What is your preferred way of expressing and experiencing love? Do you express love through kind words, physical affection, or thoughtful gestures?

*How do you show love to those closest to you? Do you wish you could express your love in a different way? If so, how do you envision expressing your love differently?*

# What are the things you value most in your relationships, both romantic and platonic?

*What are you most grateful for in the connections you have with others?*

# What are the top 10 qualities that make your spouse unique and special?

*If you are not married, you can either describe the qualities you hope to see in a future partner, or the characteristics of the loved ones in your life that you cherish.*

What is the meaning of "loyalty" to you? How do you define the boundaries of "loyalty"?

*What are the non-negotiables of loyalty for you? This applies to both romantic, and platonic relationships.*

Have you ever experienced the pain and betrayal of infidelity or an untrustworthy partner?

*If so, how did it make you feel? How did you initially react to the discovery of the infidelity? Did your response evolve over time? Did you find a way to heal and move on from this experience? If you haven't personally experienced infidelity, have you ever had someone in your life be disloyal or betray you? If so, how did it affect you, and what steps did you take toward healing and recovery?*

# What unique strengths do you bring to the table in your relationship?

*Recognize and appreciate the value that you bring to the partnership, and use this newfound understanding to enhance communication, deepen empathy, and foster trust and intimacy.*

# What qualities or characteristics do you think are essential in a "soulmate"?

*Reflect on what you think a "soulmate" is and what kind of connection you would have with your "soulmate."*

What are some things that you could do to bring more joy, connection, and intimacy into your marriage?

*If you're not married, what are some things you could do to strengthen your relationships with loved ones?*

# List 20 ways to say "I love you" through your actions.

*Sometimes actions can speak louder than words. Get creative and think outside of the box when it comes to expressing your love.*

Who do you consider your main source of support, whether it be for practical matters or emotional support?

*Think about who you can rely on for help and guidance, or who you turn to for a listening ear. It could be a family member, a friend, a spouse, or a professional like a therapist or counselor. This is a great opportunity to appreciate and acknowledge the people in your life who have been there for you and to consider how to strengthen those relationships.*

Are there people in your life who depend on you for support and guidance?

*In what ways do they rely on you? Do you enjoy being relied upon by others, or does it feel burdensome? Why do these individuals turn to you for assistance?*

What are the things that bother or upset you about your current romantic relationship?

*If you are not currently in a romantic relationship, what are the issues that cause frustration or distress in your non-romantic relationships?*

# What are the key ingredients for a "successful" and "fulfilling" marriage?

*What do you believe are the most essential elements for a strong and harmonious union? How can you work to strengthen and enhance your marriage?*

How can you use Islam to deepen your connection with your spouse and strengthen your bond?

*How much of a role does Islam currently play in your relationship? Have you had a conversation with your spouse about incorporating more spirituality into your lives? What concrete steps can you take to bring more meaning and purpose to your relationship through Islam?*

# To what extent has your upbringing shaped your marriage?

*Did your childhood experiences have a positive or negative influence on your relationship? What challenges might you face in your marriage as a result of your childhood, and how can you work to overcome them?*

# What are five of the most joyous moments you've shared with your spouse?

*What made them special for you?*

# 8
## *for*
# YOUR LEGACY

*If the Final Hour comes while you have a shoot of a plant in your hands, and it is possible to plant it before The Hour comes, you should plant it.*

—The Prophet Muhammad (peace be upon him)

The concept of success is often associated with individual achievements, but those that truly comprehend the essence of success also recognize the importance of leaving a positive impact on future generations. Success is not only about attaining our goals in this life, but also about establishing a legacy for those who will inherit the earth. The Prophet Muhammad (peace be upon him) eloquently conveyed this idea when he said: "I wish I could meet my brothers." His companions asked, "Are we not your brothers?" The Prophet (peace be upon him) replied, "You are my companions, but my brothers are those who have faith in me although they never saw me." (Musnad Aḥmad 12169) As members of the generations of Muslims who came after the passing of the revered Prophet Muhammad (peace be upon him), we are among those who never had the privilege of seeing him in the flesh, as his close companions did. Yet, it is a remarkable honor that the Prophet (peace be upon him) has been quoted as saying that he wished he could meet us. This testament to his enduring impact and legacy is a source of inspiration and motivation for us to strive towards living lives worthy of his teachings and example. This forward-thinking mindset also demonstrates that the greatest man who ever lived was constantly thinking about us and praying for us—a truly humbling thought that can only increase our love for him (peace be upon him). In a similar vein, we can find profound meaning and purpose in our own lives by considering the ripple effects of our actions and decisions on the lives of those in our community and those who will come long after us.

Our legacy is the imprint we leave behind after we bid farewell to this temporary world. It's not a matter of *if*, but *when*. And the impact we hope to make is for the benefit of future generations—not for our own glorification. The question then becomes, how can we create a lasting legacy, even if it's on just one person? Underestimating the power of our actions in this world would be a mistake. By claiming authorship over our story and offering our unique gifts to the world in a way that continues to bring goodness to others even after we're gone, we can reap the rewards of *sadaqah jaariyah*—a form of charity that brings benefits even beyond our lifetime. In this way, we can leave a legacy that is truly meaningful and stands the test of time.

As women of faith, it is important that we approach life with depth and purpose, as we are aware that death is inevitable and our connection to this world can be cut off at any moment. Thinking about the life to come and the transitory nature of this world can help us gain perspective. In this chapter, you will have the opportunity to examine your service to your community and the world at large. By the end of it, *inshaAllah,* you will have gained greater clarity and hope about your unique mission.

**Read:** "Raising Torchbearers" of *The Muslim Woman's Manifesto*

**Dua:**

رَبِّ أَوْزِعْنِى أَنْ أَشْكُرَ نِعْمَتَكَ ٱلَّتِى أَنْعَمْتَ عَلَىَّ وَعَلَىٰ وَٰلِدَىَّ وَأَنْ أَعْمَلَ صَٰلِحًا تَرْضَىٰهُ وَأَصْلِحْ لِى فِى ذُرِّيَّتِىٓ إِنِّى تُبْتُ إِلَيْكَ وَإِنِّى مِنَ ٱلْمُسْلِمِينَ

**Pronunciation:** *Rabbi auzi'ni an ashkura ni'matakal-lati an'amta 'alayya wa 'alaa waalidayya wa an a'mala solihan tardhahu wa aslih lii fii thurriyyati inni tubtu ilaika wa inni minal-muslimin*

**Meaning:** My Lord, enable me to be grateful for Your favor which You have bestowed upon me and upon my parents and to work righteousness of which You will approve and make righteous for me my offspring. Indeed, I have repented to You, and indeed, I am of the Muslims.

**Reference:** The Qur'an, 46:15

*Journaling*
PROMPTS

# Think about five people who are close to you. What qualities have you picked up from them, both good and bad?

*The people you spend time with can really shape who you are, so it's worth considering how they've influenced you.*

## How do you wish to leave your mark on the world and make a lasting impact?

*Think about the ways in which you want to be remembered and the change you want to see in the world. Also, consider the actions you take in your daily life and how they contribute to leaving a positive mark on the world. Everyone has the potential to make a difference, no matter how big or small.*

# What is one meaningful way that you can contribute to your community this month?

*Think about the unique skills and talents you possess that can be of service to those around you.*

# Write about a time when a stranger showed an act of kindness to you.

*How did it make you feel in the moment, and how has it continued to impact your life?*

# What are three of the biggest challenges you think the world is facing right now?

*How can these issues be addressed?*

# Do you see yourself to be more of a leader or a follower?

*Reflect on the reasons behind why you perceive yourself in this way.*

Many inspiring leaders are driven and dedicated to their causes. Is there a particular issue or cause that you feel deeply passionate about?

*How might you inspire others to also care about and advocate for your cause?*

# List 20 ways that you positively impact at least one other person's life?

*How do you balance the desire to positively impact others with the need to take care of yourself? How do you involve others in your efforts to positively impact others? How does positively impacting others impact your own well-being?*

Think of someone whom you deeply admire. Write a letter of gratitude to them for the influence that he or she has had on your life.

*What makes them admirable? Which quality do you share with him or her? Or which do you wish to aspire toward? You can either send this letter to the person, or you can keep it for yourself.*

How do exemplary leaders handle mistakes, and how can you learn from their example?

*See if you can find any examples from the life of the Prophet (peace be upon him) for examples of how to handle errors with grace and growth.*

# What are 10 pieces of wisdom that you would like to share with the next generation?

*The wisdom you share could be something you learned from your own experiences, or something you learned from others.*

# What are your current parenting goals?

*If you are not a parent: what values do you think are important for parents to instill in their children?*

Write a letter to your child(ren). Describe things that are most special and meaningful to you about them.

*Imagine that they will be reading this letter when they're older.*

## What are 20 lessons that you have learned from your child?

*Parenting is a two-way street, where both the parent and the child learn from each other; being a parent can be a powerful source of personal growth and self-discovery.*

# What is your approach to parenting?

*Are you more hands-on or hands-off? Do you wish your parenting style was different in any way, and if so, how?*

# How are you cultivating your child(ren)'s spiritual development?

*How do you teach them about Allah and Islam, and in what ways would you like to improve in this aspect of their upbringing? What Islamic values do you hope they will embody?*

# 9
## *for*
# THE WORLD

*You will not enter Paradise until you have faith, and you will not have faith until you love each other. Shall I show you something that, if you did, you would love each other? Spread "peace" between yourselves.*

—The Prophet Muhammad (peace be upon him)

In an age where most people are focused on what they can gain, the act of giving has become a rare and precious commodity. Interestingly, those who have less often give more, while those who have more often give less. What an interesting paradox for those who reflect!

In this chapter, we will explore the various forms of giving that go beyond material wealth. Giving can encompass all aspects of life, from the time and energy we invest in others, to simple acts of kindness such as a smile or a word of encouragement. As Muslims, we are called to be compassionate and generous towards others and this requires actively seeking opportunities to give of ourselves in meaningful ways.

Generosity is not just a religious duty, but also a way to fulfill our role as stewards of the earth. By giving of ourselves, we are able to make a positive impact on the lives of others, and in turn, our own lives are enriched. We will be discussing how giving in different forms can be an expression of gratitude, a means of forgiveness and an act of worship. It also has the power to bring people together and create a sense of community.

In this chapter, we will delve into the various ways of giving and how it can be used as a tool for personal growth, self-improvement, and spiritual fulfillment. We will also discuss the importance of being mindful of our intentions when giving, and how it can be used to purify our hearts and minds. So, let us not underestimate the power of generosity and how it can have a transformative effect on ourselves and those around us.

**Read:** "Give and You Shall Receive" from *The Muslim Woman's Manifesto*

**Dua:**

اللَّهُمَّ إِنِّي أَعُوذُ بِكَ مِنَ الْعَجْزِ وَالْكَسَلِ وَالْجُبْنِ وَالْبُخْلِ وَالْهَرَمِ وَعَذَابِ الْقَبْرِ اللَّهُمَّ آتِ نَفْسِي تَقْوَاهَا وَزَكِّهَا أَنْتَ خَيْرُ مَنْ زَكَّاهَا أَنْتَ وَلِيُّهَا وَمَوْلَاهَا اللَّهُمَّ إِنِّي أَعُوذُ بِكَ مِنْ عِلْمٍ لاَ يَنْفَعُ وَمِنْ قَلْبٍ لاَ يَخْشَعُ وَمِنْ نَفْسٍ لاَ تَشْبَعُ وَمِنْ دَعْوَةٍ لاَ يُسْتَجَابُ لَهَا

**Pronunciation:** *Allaahumma innee a`oodhu bika minal-`ajzi wal-kasal wal-jubni wal-bukhl, wal-harami wa `adhaabil-qabr. Allaahumma Aati nafsee taqwaahaa, wa zakkihaa, Anta khayru man zakkaahaa, Anta Waliyyuhaa wa Mawlaahaa. Allaahummaa innee a`oodhu bika min `ilmin laa yanfa`u, wa min qalbin laa yakh-sha`u, wa min nafsin laa tashba`u, wa min da`watin laa yustajaabu lahaa.*

**Meaning:** Oh Allah! I seek your refuge from incapacity, laziness, cowardice, miserliness, decrepit old age, and punishment of the grave. Oh Allah! Grant my soul its dutifulness (*taqwa*), and purify it, You are the One to purify it: You are its Guardian and its Lord. Oh Allah! I seek Your refuge from knowledge that does not benefit, and from a heart that is not humble, and from a soul that is never satisfied, and from a supplication that is not answered.

**Reference:** Sahih Muslim 2722

*Journaling*
PROMPTS

Think about a time when someone gave you something without expecting anything in return.

*How did it make you feel, and why do you think they did it?*

Write about a time when you faced a challenge in being generous, and how you overcame it. What did you learn from this?

*This could be a financial challenge, a personal struggle, or an external circumstance that made it difficult to give.*

# What are 10 things you can "give away" right now?

*Think about the various ways in which you can be generous, beyond just giving money. How do you give of your time, energy, or other resources to those around you?*

Identify a form of charity that you can begin practicing consistently, even if it is something small and seemingly insignificant.

*Think about something that would be easy for you to do on a regular basis and consider ways to keep it as a private and personal act of kindness.*

Is there anyone in your immediate family or social circle who is currently facing a challenge or need that you might be able to help with?

*Reflect on the various ways in which you can offer support and assistance to this person.*

# How does the act of giving make you feel emotionally and spiritually?

*Consider the feelings and emotions that arise when you give of yourself, whether it be through time, resources, or actions. It could be feelings of joy, fulfillment, or satisfaction, or it could be feelings of sacrifice, or even discomfort.*

Recall a time when you asked someone for something and they said "no." How did this make you feel, and what do you believe contributed to this emotional response?

*How did this experience help you handle "rejection" or build resilience?*

# What are 20 blessings or gifts that Allah has given to you? How can you honor each of these blessings?

*Honoring a blessing or gift can involve using it to give back to others and pay it forward.*

# What is the thing that you love the most?

*Is it a material possession, or something more abstract and profound? What makes this beloved to you, and how would you feel if you gave it away?*

# 10
## *for*
## PATIENCE

*Be patient and tough;
Someday this pain will be useful to you.*

—Ovid

Life, by its nature, involves pain and anguish. We experience trauma. Heartache. Adversity. But imagine if there was a profound wisdom underlying each and every one of those experiences? Imagine if Allah was truly using these things to test us, and ultimately bring us closer to Him? Imagine if pain was a tool that shaped us into the best version of ourselves—a bespoke chisel that etched us into a masterpiece. If we could fully understand the deeper purpose and wisdom behind our struggles, we would be overwhelmed with gratitude for the pain and hardships we face. Yes, pain hurts. But the pain of not receiving the lesson from the pain is what will hurt us the most. Pain teaches us. Pain molds us. Pain can be a powerful force that helps us grow and become stronger, but it's the lessons we learn from it that truly shape our future. Embrace the wisdom and strength gained from your struggles and use them to guide you on your journey.

In this chapter, we will delve into the heartaches and struggles that have caused us pain, and through reflection and understanding, we will seek to heal and find wisdom in these experiences. Life is often confusing and difficult to comprehend as we are living it, but by looking back and reflecting on what has passed, we can gain a deeper appreciation and understanding of its purpose. With the help of Allah, we will emerge from this chapter feeling more healed and enlightened, *inshaAllah*.

**Read:** "Be Unyielding and Resilient" of *The Muslim Woman's Manifesto*

**Dua:**

رَبَّنَا أَفْرِغْ عَلَيْنَا صَبْرًا وَثَبِّتْ أَقْدَامَنَا وَانصُرْنَا عَلَى ٱلْقَوْمِ ٱلْكَٰفِرِينَ

**Pronunciation:** *Rabbana afrigh alayna sabran wa thabbit aqdaamana wansurna alal-qawmil kaafireen*

**Meaning:** Our Lord, pour upon us patience, and make our steps firm and help us against the disbelieving people.

**Reference:** The Qur'an, 2:250

# Journaling PROMPTS

# What has been the most challenging experience or obstacle you have faced?

*What aspect of this test presented the greatest difficulty for you?*

Describe a situation that caused you to feel impatience. How did this impatience affect your thoughts and feelings, as well as your physical sensations?

*How did your impatience influence your actions and interactions with others in the moment? How has this impatience impacted you in the short and long term?*

In your day-to-day interactions with others, do you consider yourself a patient person?

*Why would being patient be a good thing for you, and for the people around you? If you do not consider yourself to be patient, in what ways could you take steps toward bettering yourself in this?*

# Are you patient with yourself and your own personal growth?

*Name a goal you're working toward, a skill you're learning, or a habit you'd like to start / have started. Are you being patient and enjoying the journey? How could practicing patience affect your overall experience?*

# What are three different ways you can react when you start feeling impatient?

*How might you practice implementing these responses to better manage your emotions in the future?*

Can you think of an example from the life of the Prophet Muhammad (peace be upon him) in which his patience was tested?

*What can we learn from this story about the importance of patience and how to cultivate it?*

Do you find that you sometimes feel impatient because you are trying to micromanage or control too many people, events, or situations in your life? What could you relinquish or let go of in order to increase your capacity for patience and peace of mind?

*If you believe that a need for control is causing you stress or difficulty, where do you think this need comes from? What steps can you take to decrease its impact on your life and increase your sense of calm and serenity?*

# How do you define "resilience"?

*What does the concept of "resilience" mean to you personally?*

What experiences or individuals in your life have helped you to develop "resilience"?

*How have these situations or people contributed to your ability to bounce back from challenges or adversity?*

Describe a difficult or challenging time in your life. What were some thoughts / actions that helped you to persevere and overcome this challenge?

*It could be something as simple as a positive attitude, the support of loved ones, or the use of effective coping mechanisms. It could also be something more complex such as seeking professional help or developing a growth mindset. Reflecting on this experience can help you understand your own resilience and strength and can provide valuable insights that can be applied to future challenges.*

# What motivates you to start your day?

*Reflecting on these factors can help you understand what drives your motivation, and how to make small adjustments to your routine that can improve your overall well-being and productivity. It can also help you identify and address any potential obstacles that may be preventing you from starting your day in a positive way.*

Can you make a list of individuals who have caused you harm or hurt your feelings, and consider ways in which you might be able to forgive them for their actions?

*Write a letter to one of the individuals who has caused you harm or hurt your feelings, expressing your forgiveness for their actions. You have the option to keep this letter private or destroy it after writing it. While forgiveness can be difficult, holding onto resentment will only hold you back. If you are not yet ready to forgive, take some time to process your feelings before revisiting this exercise.*

## What spiritual practices can you engage in to find comfort and healing during times of emotional pain or distress?

*Reflect on spiritual practices that can bring comfort and healing during times of emotional pain. Identify ways to tap into your faith for solace, support, and guidance. Find practices that work best for you and prioritize them during difficult times.*

# THE SELF-CARE TOOLKIT

There are many resources available for Muslim women experiencing mental health challenges. Some options to consider may include:

1. Muslim mental health therapists or counselors.
2. Support groups or online communities specifically for Muslim women dealing with mental health issues.
3. Mental health hotlines or crisis lines for more immediate assistance.
4. Muslim-led mental health organizations or charities.
5. Faith-based resources and support, such as imams and chaplains who can provide guidance from an Islamic perspective.

It is important to remember that seeking help for mental health issues is a sign of strength and courage—and you should never feel ashamed for doing so. When choosing a resource, make sure it feels safe and comfortable for *you*.

# TIPS FOR CHALLENGING TIMES

1. Find comfort in Allah: Your faith can be a source of strength and comfort during difficult times. Consider engaging in practices like prayer, reading the Qur'an, or seeking guidance from a person of knowledge.
2. Seek support from other Muslim women: It can be helpful to connect with other Muslim women with similar experiences. This might include joining a support group, participating in online communities, or talking to trusted friends and family members who can provide encouragement and a listening ear.
3. Remember that it's okay to ask for help: Seeking help is a sign of strength, not weakness. Don't be afraid to reach out to someone if you are struggling.
4. Practice self-compassion: It's normal to feel overwhelmed or to make mistakes during challenging times. Practice self-compassion by speaking to yourself with kindness and understanding and remember that everyone makes mistakes.
5. Take breaks: It is important to take breaks and practice self-care to help you recharge and stay focused. This might include things like getting enough sleep, eating well, and finding time for activities that make you feel happy.
6. Practice gratitude: Focusing on the things you are grateful for, even if they seem small, can help to shift your perspective, and boost your mood.
7. Take things one day at a time: It can be overwhelming to think about a difficult situation long-term. Try to focus on getting through each day and take things one step at a time.
8. Find meaning and purpose: During challenging times, it can be helpful to focus on your values and what gives your life meaning and purpose. This can help to provide a sense of direction and motivation.

**Here are some support hotlines that you can turn to if you need assistance:**

- Muslim youth helpline: 1-866-627-3342
- Muslim Crisis Text Line: Text SALAM to 741741
- Amala Muslim Youth Hopeline: Call 855-95-AMALA
- Nisa Helpline for Muslim women: 1(888)-315-NISA(6472)
- National Alliance on Mental Illness (NAMI) Helpline: 1-800-950-NAMI (6264)
- National Suicide Prevention Lifeline: 1-800-273-TALK (8255)
- Domestic Violence Hotline: 1-800-799-SAFE (7233)
- Rape, Abuse & Incest National Network (RAINN) Hotline: 1-800-656-HOPE (4673)
- The Substance Abuse and Mental Health Services Administration (SAMHSA) National Helpline: 1-800-662-HELP (4357)

*It's important to remember that these hotlines are confidential and staffed by trained professionals who can provide support, resources, and referrals.*

*Sharing your thoughts on this book, in the form of a review, would greatly benefit the author. By sharing your review, you can help ensure that this book continues to find its way into the hands of other readers to benefit from, inshaAllah. Scan the QR code to find more information on how you can support the author and this book.*

# ABOUT THE AUTHOR

Kashmir Maryam is an author, poet, and therapist-in-training who is turning heads in the literary world with her unique insights on mindfulness, spirituality, and personal growth. Born in England and of Kashmiri heritage, her books *The Muslim Woman's Manifesto: 10 Steps to Achieving Phenomenal Success, in Both Worlds*, and *Nafsi: Jihad Upon my Self* offer a fresh perspective on the intersection of spirituality and modern life. Through her guidance on self-care, inner peace, and finding purpose and meaning, she has helped countless readers discover the transformative power of personal growth and spiritual fulfilment.

In addition to her literary pursuits, Kashmir is also a passionate advocate for creative Muslim women. She co-founded Strange Inc, a nonprofit that empowers and uplifts marginalized women through coaching and educational workshops aimed at developing the skills necessary for successful publishing. With a mission to awaken the creative potential of Muslim women in a purpose-driven, spiritually aligned way, Strange Inc is fostering a new generation of community thought leaders.

*kashmirmaryam.com*
*instagram.com/kashmirmaryam*
*twitter.com/kashmirmaryam*

# MORE
*from*
# KASHMIR MARYAM

If you found this book to be a valuable resource on your journey of self-discovery and spiritual growth, you may be interested in exploring more of Kashmir's writing. Her other books offer a range of insights and inspiration that you might find enriching and helpful on your path.

### THE MUSLIM WOMAN'S MANIFESTO
10 Steps to Achieving Phenomenal Success, in Both Worlds

**This self-help book is a powerful resource for Muslim women worldwide, exploring the keys to extraordinary success. The book outlines a 10-step plan for how a faithful woman can navigate the challenges and trials of modern life while also striving to please her Creator in the hereafter. It offers practical guidance and insights for navigating the complexities of both the worldly and spiritual realms.**

*"This book is a must read! I am very picky with the type of self-help books I choose to read and there are so many reasons why this one was amazing. For one, many of the self-help books are not catered to Muslim women but this one is and helps navigate both our current life and the afterlife. I love how she talks about "middle-ground" because as a working mom who also runs her own business, things can get hectic. Today's society forces you to be one or the other but Kashmir gives you a guide on how to find balance through it all. Another important topic she touches on is how to use our time wisely. I find myself misusing my time a lot and on page 68 she uses the Fajr prayer as an example on how managing our time can be truly beneficial. Lastly, I love the action exercises because it allowed me to not only read the book and put it away. Instead, it made me dive deeper into each chapter with a goal. This book is really well written and easy to follow!"*

— Aissatou Balde, Amazon Customer

*"This book is so inspiring and has really put me in the right mindset to achieving my goals. I have been searching for a book like this but have not come across one until now. I love how this books focuses on not just this life but also the after life and how we can be successful in both worlds. I recommend everyone to read it. Being a young college student and in the process of finding/building myself this book has given me tools to find my purpose and look deeper within myself. Kashmir does an amazing job in getting you to think deeper about yourself and the world around you. Her words of wisdom will have you wanting to read more. She does an excellent job relating to her reader and includes her own personal experiences. I personally felt like this book was written for me! I also love and benefited from the exercises that are after each chapter. This book is an excellent gift for anyone looking to grow. I highly recommend!"*

—Suhaila Figueroa, Amazon Customer


*"This is such a powerful and transformative read! In this book, Kashmir Maryam eloquently discusses numerous aspects of a Muslim woman's life in such a nuanced and comprehensive way and shares insightful guidance as to how we, as Muslim women in today's world, can rise above the challenges we face by reflecting upon the teachings of the Qur'an and Hadith and properly applying these teachings to our lives as modern Muslim women.. I found this book to be extraordinarily refreshing and such a powerful guide as to how we can recalibrate our compass and reset our priorities so that we can live a fulfilling life that will allow us to thrive emotionally, personally, and professionally in this world and achieve the ultimate success in the hereafter. This is a must-read for all Muslim women trying to better understand how to live a successful, meaningful and happy life. I will definitely be recommending this book to all my friends!"*

—Meriem Djelmami-Hani, Amazon Customer

## NAFSI
### Jihad Upon My Self

**Nafsi is a collection of poetry and prose, calling you to a spiritual revolution. This compelling work examines the conflict between the soul and the body – its desires, its pain, its love, and its hope. Through poetic allure, this collection will speak directly to your soul, in a way that is hauntingly beautiful.**

*"An absolute masterpiece! In itself, this collection is a work of art. It will break you down then put you back together."*
—Adam Haris, President and Founder of portalislam.net

*"Kashmir shares the pain, trauma, confusion and love within the hearts of Muslims everywhere through words that seep deep into the pores of humanity. Her words are heartbreaking, yet hopeful. She pens our inner conflicts on paper as a remedy for healing of all people. If you want to feel understood, read "Nafsi'."*
—Linda Sarsour, an Award-winning American Muslim Racial Justice and Civil Rights Activist from New York City

*"The voice of the poetess soars in this very spiritual collection of verse. In a time of war for liberation, Kashmir Maryam sets herself to the vital task of freeing our Selves from their enslavement to earthly desires. This debut publication is a testament to the vision and ability of an already accomplished artist, one we hope will continue to inspire ethical resistance and community reflection among the people of faith and conscience."*
—Cyrus McGoldrick, Author of "I of the Garden"

Made in the USA
Coppell, TX
14 February 2025